C. 1

JB
Knight
Vasco da Gama

	DATE DUE		
8/18			

Vasco da Gama

by David Knight
illustrated by George Sottung

Troll Associates

Troll Associates, Mahwah, N.J.
Library of Congress Catalog Card Number: 78-18057
ISBN 0-89375-175-8
ISBN 0-89375-167-7 Paper Edition

Vasco da Gama

Fourteen-year-old Vasco da Gama took the steering oar of Pedro Vasquez's fishing boat and headed out into the bay. Pedro was an old family friend, and Vasco often went fishing with him. It was Pedro who had taught Vasco how to handle the boat.

The boy watched the large three-cornered sail fill with wind. The mast tipped slightly as the boat creaked and groaned. Then the boat suddenly shot forward through the water. Vasco was sailing now—and it was what he loved to do best!

5

He glanced back over his shoulder at the small town along the sunny Portuguese coast. Sines was his home—he had been born there in about 1460. Up on the hill rose the thick white walls of the fortress that protected the town. His father, a nobleman of high rank, was its commander. Vasco's grandfathers also had been soldiers. But Vasco had decided long ago that he would become a sailor—someday he would command his own ship.

6

Then Vasco caught sight of a large ship in the distance. Pedro saw it, too. All of its white sails were set and pulling hard. Pennants fluttered from the tops of the masts.

"A pretty sight, is she not?" asked old Pedro.

"Yes. . ." Vasco agreed thoughtfully. "Perhaps *that* will be the ship, Pedro."

"What do you mean, Vasco?"

"I mean," said Vasco, slowly, "that it may be the ship that finds the sea route around Africa to the Indies."

"Perhaps," murmured Pedro, "and perhaps not."

To prepare himself for a sailor's life, Vasco was already taking lessons in mathematics and navigation. He knew that the ships of Portugal were pushing farther and farther down the coast of Africa to trade and explore. He dreamed of sailing aboard one of them some day.

The boy gazed at the ship and thought of his hero, Prince Henry the Navigator. He had died about the same time Vasco had been born. Henry, a prince of Portugal, had spent most of his life planning expeditions of discovery. He had wanted to find out about every part of the world beyond Europe—especially the East. He believed that his captains could find a route around Africa . . . then sail eastward until they reached the far-off lands of Asia, which Europeans called the *Indies*.

Vasco remembered Prince Henry's reasons for wanting to find a sea route. Hundreds of years before, in the time of their great leader, Mohammed, the Arabs had conquered the cities along the east coast of Africa. Then they had built up a rich trade with India.

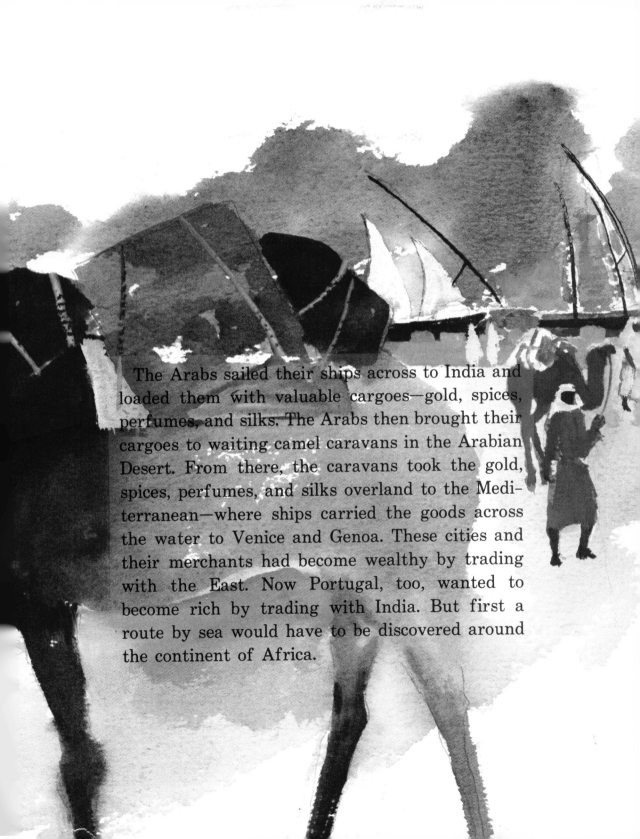

The Arabs sailed their ships across to India and loaded them with valuable cargoes—gold, spices, perfumes, and silks. The Arabs then brought their cargoes to waiting camel caravans in the Arabian Desert. From there, the caravans took the gold, spices, perfumes, and silks overland to the Mediterranean—where ships carried the goods across the water to Venice and Genoa. These cities and their merchants had become wealthy by trading with the East. Now Portugal, too, wanted to become rich by trading with India. But first a route by sea would have to be discovered around the continent of Africa.

Unfortunately, Prince Henry had died without seeing any of his captains find such a route. His explorers sailed south—past the Cape Verde Islands, and along the west coast of Africa. But they never sailed far enough. Now, years after Prince Henry's death, nobody had yet reached the southern end of Africa. Perhaps the great navigator had been wrong. In his heart, however, Vasco believed that somehow Prince Henry had been right. After all, Africa had to end *somewhere*.

13

A year later, when Vasco was 15, he got the chance to go to sea. Very little is known about his early voyages. But it is known that he sailed and often traded in the ports along the western coast of Africa.

A seafaring man in Vasco da Gama's time had to be brave and skillful. During storms at sea, the wild, thundering waves of the Atlantic Ocean piled up as high as mountains. They could crush the tiny, high-decked sailing ships of that day like matchwood. A frightened sailor who lost his grip on a line or a spar could be swept overboard in seconds.

14

Many ships were blown off course and were
never seen again. And navigating these little ships
was very difficult. Compasses and other in-
struments used for steering were crude and not
very accurate. So a good sea captain had to know
the stars well—and how to steer his ship by them.
He had to have good sense and good judgment—
about his ship, his crew, and the sea.

The captains that da Gama sailed for liked the serious young sailor. They noticed that da Gama was not afraid during the howling storms at sea. When he took his turn at the ship's wheel, he steered a straight, steady course. He did not complain about the long, dangerous hours up in the rigging, setting and rolling up the heavy canvas sails. He knew the stars well and could steer by them. These captains talked about da Gama to the merchants whose ships they sailed. Soon Vasco da Gama was given ships of his own to command. In his early twenties, he had become a captain himself.

Da Gama had changed considerably from the boy who had sailed old Pedro's boat off Sines. Years of hard work at sea had made him very strong. He was deeply tanned, with a dark beard that framed his mouth. As a ship's captain, he knew well the loneliness that came with command. His crews found him a silent, strict leader—one who sometimes lost his temper but who was usually fair.

18

During these years, it is not certain how far down the African coast da Gama sailed. But it is sure that he had not forgotten Prince Henry's dream of a sea route around the tip of Africa to the East.

It was not Vasco da Gama, however, who first rounded the tip of Africa. It was a fellow countryman, Captain Bartholomew Dias, who did it by accident in 1488. Dias had pushed his ships far down the west coast of Africa. Suddenly, a violent storm swept them down beyond the end of the continent. When the storm was over, Dias steered eastward, thinking he would find the west coast again. He found nothing but water. Then he steered northward until he saw land. Realizing he must now be on the *east* coast of Africa, Dias wanted to sail on toward India. But his men threatened to mutiny—to take over the ships—and Dias had to sail back to Lisbon. There he told King John what had happened.

The king was pleased. Now it had been proved that a ship could sail around Africa. But for several years, he delayed sending expeditions to the East. For one thing, King John feared trouble with other nations if Portugal started to trade with the East. Also, most seamen of his day were afraid to sail in uncharted seas. They believed in sea serpents and other monsters—such as whales so large they were able to swallow ships whole. He knew it would be difficult to find crews willing to go on the long voyage into the unknown waters around the tip of Africa.

Almost ten years after Dias' voyage, King John at last decided to send Portuguese ships to India. He considered several able men to lead the expedition, including Bartholomew Dias. He also considered Vasco da Gama—perhaps the best sea captain Portugal had. Then the king died. The new king, Manuel, went ahead with King John's plans. He ordered ships to be built immediately, with da Gama as captain.

Although Bartholomew Dias was disappointed not to be commanding the expedition, he proved to be of great help to da Gama in preparing the ships. Together, the two men designed a vessel better able to withstand the high winds and battering seas around the Cape of Good Hope, as King John had named the tip of Africa.

Dias also gave da Gama expert sailing advice. He knew that along the coastline of west Africa, the winds and currents would work against the ships. He told da Gama to steer wide of the coast and out into the open Atlantic for more favorable winds.

23

When they were ready, Captain da Gama's new ships made a fine-looking fleet. They were well stocked with food, water, and other supplies. Da Gama wanted to be prepared for a long and difficult voyage. His flagship was the *São Gabriel*. Two other ships in the fleet were the *São Rafael* and the *Berrio*. A fourth, larger vessel, the *São Maria*, was taken along as a storeship.

It took months to recruit the crew of about 150 men. A few signed up because they were truly excited at the idea of a voyage of discovery. But most were hardened, tough sailors who knew no other life. There were even a few convicts among them. They had been promised their freedom if they survived the expedition. Many of the sailors were frightened at the thought of sailing into the unknown waters on the other side of Africa.

The fleet sailed from Lisbon on July 8, 1497. Heading down the west coast of Africa, the ships stopped briefly at the Cape Verde Islands to take on food and water. Once below the Equator, da Gama took Bartholomew Dias' advice and turned away from the coastline and out into the open sea. For many days, captain and crew saw nothing but water. But as Dias had promised, they eventually picked up the favorable trade winds. Da Gama's fleet was soon racing toward the tip of Africa.

It wasn't until November 7 that the sailors saw land again. They anchored for a few days at Santa Helena Bay and then sailed on. In spite of fierce winds, da Gama's ships finally fought their way around the stormy Cape of Good Hope on November 22. Three days later, they dropped anchor east of the Cape.

Here, as was the custom, da Gama erected a *padrão*—a stone pillar—as proof of his discovery. A few days before Christmas, da Gama spotted another padrão, the last one that his friend Dias had put up. Da Gama now knew he was about to sail in waters never before entered by any other European.

On Christmas Day—without the storeship, which was destroyed—da Gama's fleet reached the African province of Natal. But by now, a disease called *scurvy* had broken out among the ships' crews. Caused by a lack of fresh fruit and vegetables in their diet, this illness greatly weakened the men. Sailors' flesh turned black, their teeth fell out, and their arms and legs swelled painfully. Many of the crewmen died before the disease had run its course.

But da Gama continued up the east African coast. Then, on March 2, 1498, the fleet sailed into the large harbor of Mozambique. This important trading center was controlled by the Arabs. They did not want to share the rich trade of the East with Portugal or any other nation. Seeing da Gama's sails, the Arabs were immediately suspicious of these European ships in their harbor.

To make matters worse, when the Arab ruler of Mozambique came aboard the flagship *São Gabriel*, he expected to be honored with valuable gifts. But da Gama had not thought to bring along such things. All he could give the ruler were trinkets and clothing. The ruler went ashore, greatly insulted. "These Portuguese," he muttered. "They seek to take over the world. This cannot be allowed to happen."

The situation soon grew worse. Much of this was da Gama's own fault. He wished to impress the Arabs with his power. When they refused to let his sailors go ashore to get water, da Gama lost his temper. He fired at the Arabs and killed some of them. Finally, after a month of fighting, da Gama sailed out of Mozambique. He had only succeeded in giving the Arabs on the east coast of Africa further reason to hate the Portuguese.

A week later, da Gama's ships entered the harbor of another Arab town—Mombasa. But the sultan of Mombasa had gotten word that da Gama was on his way, and he had laid a trap. Offering fresh fruit and meat, he tried to get da Gama to sail into the inner harbor. There he could easily destroy the enemy ships. But da Gama was suspicious, and stayed outside. Late at night, two boatloads of Arabs rowed out to the *Berrio*. Climbing quietly aboard, they began cutting up the ship's sails and rigging. But the alarm was given in time, and the *Berrio*'s crew was able to drive off the invaders. The next morning, da Gama wisely set sail and left Mombasa.

The fleet continued up the coast for another 30 miles. Here Captain da Gama dropped anchor at what was to be his last port of call on the African coast. This was Malindi. The ruler of Malindi was an enemy of the sultan of Mombasa, so he welcomed da Gama and his men. Da Gama, eager now to cross the great Indian Ocean, asked for a pilot who knew those waters well. "I can provide you with the best," the ruler said. "His name is Ahmad. He knows the Malabar Coast of India well. It is the richest region in that country."

On April 24, 1498, the ships sailed out of Malindi.
Soon Africa was far behind them. Ahmad made
skillful use of the monsoon winds. At that time of
year, they blew steadily from Africa to India. The
ships moved rapidly eastward. After 23 days at
sea, lookouts in the rigging spotted land. Ahmad
informed da Gama that this was the Indian coast
of Malabar, and he piloted the ships safely into the
port city of Calicut. Gratefully, da Gama wrote in
his journal: "God be thanked that our outward
voyage is done."

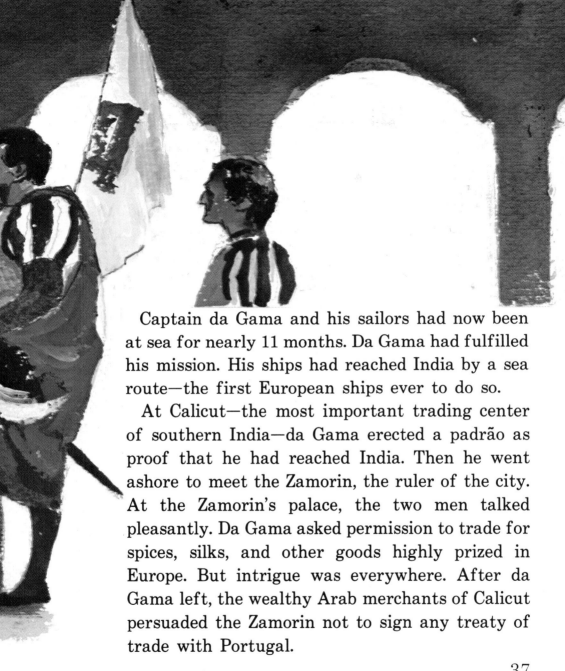

Captain da Gama and his sailors had now been at sea for nearly 11 months. Da Gama had fulfilled his mission. His ships had reached India by a sea route—the first European ships ever to do so.

At Calicut—the most important trading center of southern India—da Gama erected a padrão as proof that he had reached India. Then he went ashore to meet the Zamorin, the ruler of the city. At the Zamorin's palace, the two men talked pleasantly. Da Gama asked permission to trade for spices, silks, and other goods highly prized in Europe. But intrigue was everywhere. After da Gama left, the wealthy Arab merchants of Calicut persuaded the Zamorin not to sign any treaty of trade with Portugal.

Influenced by the jealous Arab merchants, the Zamorin demanded that the Portuguese leave Calicut. Then the trouble began. The townspeople mocked da Gama's sailors on the streets. There was fighting and bloodshed.

On August 29, the day da Gama sailed from Calicut, several boatloads of Arabs attacked his ships. Da Gama fired on them with his deck cannon and sank some of the boats. Leaving India behind him, he headed his ships westward—toward home.

The monsoon winds had not yet shifted in his favor. So it took nearly three months to re-cross the Indian Ocean! Again the dreaded disease of scurvy broke out, and before it was over, many sailors had died.

Da Gama soon realized that he did not have enough men left to handle all three ships. So he beached the *São Rafael* on the east coast of Africa and then set the ship afire. On March 20, 1499, the *São Gabriel*, da Gama's flagship, and the *Berrio* at last rounded the Cape of Good Hope. From there, a fine breeze pushed them up the African coast toward Portugal.

On September 9, 1499, da Gama's two small ships sailed into Lisbon. Spectators could see how weatherbeaten the vessels were. They stared at the weak, ragged men working on deck. There were only about 70 of them—all that were left of the 150 who had set sail over two years before. They and their captain had sailed almost 24,000 miles.

All Lisbon turned out to welcome the heroes back home. Word had quickly spread that Captain da Gama had succeeded in discovering the long-sought sea route to India. In doing this, he had performed great feats of seamanship and navigation.

44

Even though trade agreements were still not signed, da Gama's voyage was considered a great triumph. Portugal was now in a position to compete with the Arabs, and could look forward to a thriving trade with the East—and certain wealth. Indeed, all Europe would eventually benefit from da Gama's discoveries. King Manuel was delighted with da Gama's success. He honored the explorer by making him a nobleman, and gave him more than enough money to live on for the rest of his life.

Two years later, in 1502, King Manuel sent Vasco da Gama on a second trip to India. Before he sailed, the king named da Gama an Admiral of India. And a few months later, he returned to Lisbon with a favorable trade treaty in his pocket!

Years later, in 1524, da Gama was again sent to India—this time as Royal Governor. On Christmas Eve of that year, the aging explorer died in the far-off land he had first sighted over twenty-five years before.